MAKER OF MACHINES

A Creative Minds Biography

MAKER OF MACHINES

A Story about Eli Whitney

by Barbara Mitchell

illustrations by Jan Naimo Jones

Carolrhoda Books, Inc./Minneapolis

For my brother George
In celebration of Cornog Pattern Company—B.M.

With special thanks to my parents, who always
encouraged the creative part of me—Jan

Text copyright © 2004 by Barbara Mitchell
Illustrations copyright © 2004 by Jan Naimo Jones

This book is available in two editions:
Library binding by Carolrhoda Books, Inc.,
   a division of Lerner Publishing Group
Soft cover by First Avenue Editions,
   an imprint of Lerner Publishing Group
241 First Avenue North
Minneapolis, MN 55401 U.S.A.

Website address: www.lernerbooks.com

Library of Congress Cataloging-in-Publication Data

Mitchell, Barbara, 1941–
     Maker of machines : a story about Eli Whitney / by Barbara Mitchell ;
  illustrations by Jan Naimo Jones.
       p.   cm. — (A creative minds biography)
     Includes bibliographical references and index.
     Contents: Boy with an idea—Machines, machines—It's got teeth—
  Calamity after calamity—Muskets for America—Man of ideas.
     ISBN: 1–57505–603–8 (lib. bdg. : alk. paper)
     ISBN: 1–57505–634–8 (pbk. : alk. paper)
     1. Whitney, Eli, 1765–1825—Juvenile literature. 2. Inventors—United
  States—Biography—Juvenile literature. 3. Mass production—United
  States—History—Juvenile literature. 4. Muzzle-loading firearms—
  Juvenile literature. [1. Whitney, Eli, 1765–1825. 2. Inventors.] I. Jones,
  Jan Naimo, ill. II. Title. III. Series.
  TS1570.W4M58 2004
  609.2—dc21   2003010551

Manufactured in the United States of America
1 2 3 4 5 6 – JR – 09 08 07 06 05 04

Table of Contents

1

Boy with an Idea

In the springtime of 1776, a boy named Eli Whitney and a Connecticut Colony lawyer named Silas Deane both had big ideas. Deane arrived at the royal court of France that spring. He had come all the way across the Atlantic Ocean to buy muskets for America. The American colonies, ruled by mighty Great Britain, were going to war for their freedom.

But makers of the long-barreled guns carried by soldiers were scarce in the colonies, Deane said. Led by General George Washington, the soldiers fighting against the British redcoats had hardly a musket.

A court attendant stood listening. His heart went out to the Americans. Fighting a war without guns would be most difficult. French gunsmiths made muskets by the thousands, with a new model every few years. The Royal Arsenal at Charleville was overflowing with old muskets. But would the king of France give muskets to colonists who were rebelling against another king? Not likely. A sorry situation it was for those brave Americans with nary a musket maker to be had.

Back in the American colony of Massachusetts, ten-year-old Eli Whitney was thinking too. He was also feeding his father's cows. But to Eli, the best thing about forking food and toting buckets of water to sixty cattle was that it gave him plenty of time to ponder. Eli loved to ponder, turning ideas over and over in his mind.

Eli was not much for farmwork. He would far rather be in the farm's pine-smelling workshop, thinking up something to make. And if he wasn't hammering and chiseling some creation with his father's tools, why then he was pulling something apart to see what made it work. This morning Eli had his mind set on disassembling a curious little machine called a pocket watch. There was a brand-new one in Father's dresser drawer.

Springtime turned to summer. The American colonies declared themselves free of Great Britain forever. "HUZZAH! HUZZAH!" people in Eli's hometown of Westborough, Massachusetts, cried. "HURRAY! HURRAY!"

But freedom had only been declared. It was not yet won. Day after day, new volunteers for General Washington's army tramped the dusty road that passed the Whitney farm. The neighbors-turned-soldiers carried turkey-shooting guns, some of them as old as one hundred years. Only a smattering of the soldiers shouldered better-quality, newly made Brown Bess muskets like the ones the redcoats had. Eli took notice of that.

A new musket cost a year's wages, colonists in Westborough said, if there were one to be found. There was no rushing the making of a musket. Every one of its fifty pieces was made by hand. What would happen? Eli wondered. Would the fight for freedom be lost for lack of muskets?

The following winter, three French ships appeared off the Atlantic coast. Smuggled deep in their holds were 30,000 muskets. The faraway French court attendant had convinced the king to get rid of these older guns. One ship did not make it past the British warships standing guard. But the other two arrived safely at American ports. They brought 23,000 long-barreled muskets, stamped "Charleville 1763," to George Washington's soldiers.

Freedom fighting was hard work. It took a toll on the muskets as the war went on. A year passed by, and then another. The guns from France were sadly in need of repair. General Washington sent out an order saying that all muskets must be kept in full working order at all times. Gunsmiths being scarce, fixing the muskets' iron parts became the job of local blacksmiths.

Farms around Westborough began to show signs of needing repair. The farmers could not get nails. Nails had once come from Great Britain, but the war had closed the harbors. Farmers had to go to blacksmiths for nails. But blacksmiths had no time for hammering out nails, they told the farmers. They were busy fixing General Washington's muskets.

The farmers were annoyed. Just how were they to grow food for the soldiers if they had no nails to keep their barns and equipment in shape? Requests from General Washington had gone out to farmers as well as to blacksmiths. States were not sending enough food to the troops. Soldiers were living on horse feed and pumpkin shells.

The problem gave Eli an idea. The idea followed

him in and out of the stalls of sixty chomping cows as he did his chores. By the time he sat down to dinner with his family, the idea was whirling like a snow-storm in his mind. Nails! He would make nails for the American Revolution.

Eli had it all worked out. First, he would have to convince his father that he could hammer out a nail. That was the thing about nails. Eli had never actually made one. He believed that he could, though. Secondly, he would have to persuade Father to put in a forge. Installing the fiery furnace for heating iron so that it could be softened and shaped into nails would cost money.

It was that second part that would be tough. Father already had enough problems to worry about. Eli's gentle mother had never regained her strength follow-ing the birth of Josiah, Eli's youngest brother. In the summer of 1777, she had passed away, leaving the family—Eli, his brothers Benjamin and Josiah, and their sister Elizabeth—alone. Then Father had remar-ried. There were two new stepsisters to provide for, as well.

Eli spent more and more time in the pine-smelling workshop. Thinking up things to make helped soften the sadness of losing his mother. Father had even begun letting him use the lathe. This fast-turning machine shaped spindles and legs for Whitney-made chairs, which were sold all over Westborough.

Finally, Eli told his father about the great idea. Nails would keep the farmers' tools and barns in repair, Eli argued. (Eli was very good at arguing.) The farmers would feed General Washington's army. And to top it off, Eli would make money. A good nailer could turn out 3,000 nails a day. The forge would soon pay for itself.

Mr. Whitney pondered the situation. Shaping a four-sided nail from a piece of white-hot iron took skill. But he knew that Eli could do it. His son had mastered the lathe, had he not? If Eli could shape delicate chair parts on that fast-turning machine, then surely he could hammer out nails. It was a deal, Father said. He would install the forge. Eli would do the work.

Fourteen-year-old Eli's nail business was such a success that by the second winter he needed to hire a helper. Then in 1781, the war ended. The colonies had won their freedom from Great Britain. There was peace. Harbors were open to ships again, ships that dumped cheap British nails onto American docks. Making nails was no longer profitable. That did not bother Eli. He would simply come up with another business idea.

The British ships carried the latest in ladies' hat styles from London and Paris. Eli stared at the huge puffs of bonnets, covered with jewels and lace. How in the world did the gigantic coverings remain on ladies' heads? he wondered. The stylish new bonnets were "pind," Elizabeth said, with three long hatpins.

Hatpins! Eli would make women's hatpins. There was sure to be a profit in that. Drawing the iron out into slim pins for bonnets would be more difficult than shaping nails. No matter. He would simply keep trying until it was done. And if hatpins should go out of fashion, why then, he would go back to the lathe and make gentlemen's canes.

There was a reason Eli worked so hard and saved every bit of money he earned. Whirling in his mind was another idea. This one was so big that it was months before he dared to mention it—even to Elizabeth. Her brother was planning to go to college, Elizabeth soon learned. And not to just any college. Eli had his heart set on going to Yale.

Eli knew that passing the entrance tests for the fine school in New Haven, Connecticut, would be difficult. He would have to prove that he could read Latin and Greek. His skills in mathematics and English grammar would have to be far greater than those provided by the country schoolhouse he had attended.

It would all mean going to nearby Leicester Academy before he could even think of sitting in a Yale classroom. The academy was a private school. It would cost money. So Eli got a job as a schoolmaster in a neighboring town for seven dollars a month. He also found someone to help him with his math lessons. His tutor, Elizur Goodrich, was one of the finest mathematics teachers in America. His son, Elizur Jr., was Eli's age. Elizur Jr. and Eli were soon friends.

Then came Eli's biggest challenge of all—asking his parents to help him with the money for Yale. It was his stepmother he worried over most. The new Mrs. Whitney always seemed to be worried about money. She did not seem to understand Eli's need to be involved with things of the mind.

Father understood. But college bills had to be paid on schedule. Otherwise, a student would be asked to leave. Suppose the crops failed one season? Father asked. He might have to break his promise. Mr. Whitney was proud to be known as a man who kept his word.

Mr. Whitney looked into his son's dark, pleading eyes. Times were hard for farmers since the war, he explained gently.

Please, Eli begged. The money would only be a loan. When he graduated from Yale, he would pay it all back.

2

Machines, Machines

Eli Whitney took the entrance test for Yale College on April 30, 1789, the day George Washington became the first president of the United States of America. He was admitted to the school that very afternoon. The new Yale freshman was twenty-three years old. He was already behind. Most students entered college at fourteen or fifteen.

It had taken Eli long winters of teaching in one-room schoolhouses to earn the money for his education. Along with what was left of his small teacher's salary came a promise from his father. Mr. Whitney would send money whenever he was able. But many times, no money arrived. So Eli took little jobs around town. He worked as a carpenter's helper. He colored maps for students in his geography class for one dollar per set.

One of Eli's favorite spots was the college's "table of curiosities." Yale professors used the table's tools for teaching science.

These tools included a set of simple machines: a pulley, a lever, an inclined plane, a wedge, a screw, and a toothed wheel. Eli had used tools like these for building things in his father's workshop. His professors used them to teach students about the scientific laws at work in each machine.

Eli had never heard of some machines, such as a theodolite for measuring angles and a micrometer for measuring tiny distances. He was especially fascinated by a machine called an orrery that showed the movement of the planets. It was not so much the solar system that intrigued Eli as the clockworks that made the machine go. If only he could take that orrery apart!

Machines were in the news too. Inventors in Great Britain had created machines for spinning and weaving cotton. A British mechanic who had moved to America had built one of these spinning machines from memory. A cotton mill with the new machine was going up nearby in Rhode Island.

Whispery soft cotton cloth, available only from India by way of British ships, would soon be made right here in the United States. The Yale boys, for their part, were rejoicing. The only cotton they knew about was itchy linsey-woolsey, made of wool and rough cotton or linen. The coats and trousers that students had to wear were made of the scratchy cloth.

But the mill owner was paying a hefty tax on the cotton he imported from the West Indies. Planters along the Georgia and South Carolina seacoasts were growing cotton as an experiment. One question hung heavy in the air. Should America be making machines to produce its own cotton clothing?

Debating timely questions was an important subject at Yale. The school was known for graduating lawyers. Every student had to write persuasive essays and defend his point of view before the other students. Eli's papers asked questions such as "Should America make its own products, in order to be truly free of Great Britain?" and "Does the new nation's security depend upon developing its own way of making things?" These questions fascinated Eli. He enjoyed taking apart ideas almost as much as he enjoyed taking apart machines. He began to think about becoming a lawyer.

Then a former student named Phineas Miller came to find a private teacher for the children of a wealthy South Carolina family. Ezra Stiles, Yale's president, recommended Eli for the job. Eli could earn money to pay back his father and begin studying law at the same time, President Stiles suggested.

Eli graduated from Yale in 1792 and headed south for his new job. But the venture went badly from the start. Eli took a boat to Georgia with Phineas and Mrs. Catherine Greene. Catherine—nicknamed Kitty—was the widow of one of George Washington's generals. She owned a large plantation, or southern-style farm, called Mulberry Grove near Savannah, Georgia. Phineas was the plantation's manager.

Eli planned to enjoy a relaxing sail south along the Atlantic coast to Savannah with Phineas and Kitty. Then he would ride a riverboat across the Savannah River to South Carolina. But he was seasick all the way. And when he arrived in South Carolina, he learned there had been a misunderstanding. The teaching job paid much less than he had thought. There was no way Eli could get by on the small amount of money, especially when he had to pay back his father.

Kitty Greene invited him to stay at Mulberry Grove until he knew what he was going to do next. Eli accepted. He happily fixed tools, repaired toys for Kitty's five children, and made himself useful around the house and plantation.

Talk at Mulberry Grove was all about cotton. Plantation owners were worried. Years of planting tobacco had taken the minerals from their soil. Tobacco no longer earned enough money to keep the big farms going. The owners could not even afford to keep the slaves who worked the land, even though their only pay was a little food and clothing. The answer was cotton, the farmers said. British factories were hungry for it. And there was that new cotton mill, full of spinning machines, up in Rhode Island.

There was a problem, however, Kitty's neighbors explained to Eli. The black-seed cotton being grown in the sandy soil of Georgia's seacoast would not grow in inland soil. Planters were experimenting with green-seed cotton. But the new cotton was difficult to clean. Slaves painstakingly pulled the fluffs of cotton fibers, called bolls, from the green, sticky seeds. At the end of a ten-hour day, each worker ended up with sore fingers . . . and just one pound of seedless cotton.

They had tried to remove the pesky seeds using roller gins, the planters told Eli. The gins used a pair of grooved rollers, turned by a crank, to squash the cotton and rub the seeds out. Roller gins worked just fine on smooth black-seed cotton. But on furry green-seed cotton, they were no good at all. If only a clever inventor could come up with a better gin, the cotton growers said. Surely that would be good for America. And for the inventor too, they added.

Eli had never seen a roller gin. He had never even seen a boll of cotton. But he could learn. Eli took a fluffy pod of cotton in his hand. With the fingers of his other hand, he pulled as hard as he could, just as the slaves did. The seeds in their sticky green coats clung to the wooly cotton fibers, like burrs in a dog's coat. Eli pulled again. The seeds refused to budge.

The problem gave Eli an idea. Cotton cleaning was a job that needed mechanical hands, hands that could work like human hands, only better. The cotton planters needed a machine.

Eli believed that he could make that machine. Just ten days later, he had a model built. Eli had made a wooden box with a crank on the side. A curved iron grate in the middle of the box held the cotton. To do the work of pulling fingers, Eli had made a roller studded with iron teeth.

When Eli turned the crank, the roller turned too. Its teeth combed between the slots in the grate. The tooth-fingers pulled the cotton fibers through the grate and onto the roller. But the slots were too small for the seeds to pass through. They stayed on the other side of the grate. Then—plop! Those pesky seeds fell into the box below.

But after just a few turns of the crank—CHONK—the little engine jammed. The roller collecting the cleaned cotton looked like a sheep badly in need of a haircut. Somehow, Eli needed to clear away the col-lected fibers.

And there was another problem. Eli planned to cut the teeth from metal. But he could not find the special sheets of iron that he needed. What could he use?

Eli thought hard. Then he remembered that one of Mrs. Greene's daughters had brought him a coil of wire, asking the family's clever visitor to make a birdcage for her. There the young Miss Greene had stood with a coil of nice thin wire in her hands. There Eli now sat in the quiet of Mrs. Greene's parlor, pondering his problem. An idea struck him. He could make wire teeth for his cotton cleaner.

The whole winter long, Eli worked on his machine. He forgot all about becoming a teacher or a lawyer. By April 1793, his secret workroom in the Greene basement held a bigger and better cotton gin. The new model had delicate, hooklike teeth. It also had a second roller, set with bristles like a brush. When Eli turned the crank, both rollers turned. The roller with the brush turned four times faster, and in the opposite direction, than the roller that collected the cotton fibers. WHOOSH! The cleaned cotton was whisked away by the bristles. The invention worked.

Eli joyfully reported the news to his father. He had invented a machine! With his cotton gin, a single person would be able to clean ten times as much cotton as ever had been done before.

Eli's invention was sure to be profitable. He would pay back his father in no time. But he was worried that somebody might steal his idea. Mr. Whitney was not to tell a soul outside the family, his son the inventor cautioned.

The popular Kitty Greene, though, was all for telling the world. Best not do that until he could register the invention with the U.S. Patent Office, Eli cautioned. The patent office in Philadelphia, the nation's capital, was new. It had been set up to encourage invention in America and to protect inventors from having their ideas stolen. Thomas Jefferson, President Washington's secretary of state, was in charge.

She had already shown some friends into the secret workroom, Mrs. Greene confessed, just a couple of planters. Surely she had done no harm?

Quickly, Eli got ready for a trip to Philadelphia.

3

It's Got Teeth

On the first of June, Eli boarded a boat to carry him back up the Atlantic coast. What was a bit of seasickness? The future of his invention was at stake.

The boat docked in New York City. Eli planned to buy tools and materials there, in order to set up a workshop for building cotton gins. But first he had to take care of the urgent paperwork needed to protect his invention.

Boarding a stagecoach, Eli hurried off to Philadelphia and the patent office. On June 20, he filed his patent application, along with the required payment and a personal letter to Thomas Jefferson. To Eli's disappointment, he did not get to meet the famous Jefferson, author of the Declaration of Independence. A clerk took his application and advised the inventor to go home and await a reply.

Eli returned to New York the very next day. There was shopping to do!

Back in the busy port city, he bought the special tools and supplies that he would need. He bought pliers for cutting, files for polishing, and ninety-six pounds of iron wire for making teeth. Most of the other tools Eli needed—such as a machine for making screws, a lathe, and a tool for making the wire even thinner—he would build himself.

Then Eli got right to work on the next step of his patent application, which was to prepare drawings and a detailed description of his machine. He hoped to send them to Thomas Jefferson within a few weeks. But an outbreak of yellow fever in Philadelphia slowed things down. The disease put a stop to business in the city and held up the mail. Finally, on October 15, 1793, Eli sent the papers off to Jefferson, eager for his response.

Thomas Jefferson spent his days working in Philadelphia's stately government buildings. But he was really a Virginia plantation owner at heart. And he was also an inventor. He was full of questions for Eli in his November 16 letter. Had the machine been well tested? On average, how much cotton would it clean in three days' time? Was it practical for people to use at home? If Mr. Whitney's ingenious machine really worked, Jefferson wanted one for himself.

Eli wrote back immediately. His machine was like no other, he declared. In two weeks of testing, a single worker had turned out 60 to 80 pounds of cleaned cotton per day (from 180 to 190 pounds of picked cotton). The machine could be made small, taking up only a few feet of space, and was most certainly practical for home use. Gins three times that size could be made as well.

Normally, an inventor would have a long wait for his application to go through the government. But Jefferson made sure that Eli's application moved right ahead. All Whitney had yet to do, said Jefferson, was send a small copy of the machine to be kept by the government.

To make the little model, and to make full-sized gins later, Eli had already begun setting up shop in New Haven, Connecticut. He had hired mechanics and carpenters. Phineas had agreed to be his business partner. Running a business with one partner in the North and the other in the South would be hard. But skilled workers were scarce in the South.

To stock his workshop, Eli bought wood, hammers, saws, chisels, sandpaper, and glue. Last of all, he bought a big brass key to lock the secret workshop and a broom for keeping it tidy. All was ready. He could truly get down to work. First, he would build the model gin for the patent office, perfect in every detail. Then it would be on to making the real thing—full-size gins and lots of them. They would have turning rollers five feet long, covered with hundreds of wires set at a carefully figured angle.

In February 1794, Eli took the stagecoach back to Philadelphia. The perfect little cotton gin lay safely in his lap. He could hardly wait to show the beautifully made machine to Thomas Jefferson. With his love of inventions, the secretary of state was sure to be pleased.

But Jefferson was no longer secretary of state, Eli learned. He had returned to his plantation. Eli had missed meeting the famous Virginian inventor again. Disappointed, he left his model with Oliver Wolcott, the secretary of the U.S. Treasury. Eli returned to New Haven.

On March 6, an advertisement placed by Phineas Miller appeared in the *Gazette of the State of Georgia*. According to the newspaper notice, a business known as Miller and Whitney would be placing gins for cleaning cotton in various parts of the country in time for the upcoming harvest. Miller and Whitney would clean any amount of cotton, the article said. The only payment need be a portion of the crop.

The fact that machines for cleaning cotton were about to sprout up all over the countryside was news to the state of Georgia. It was news to Eli, as well. Officially, Miller and Whitney did not yet exist. Eli and Phineas had not yet signed the papers to make the business legal. In reality, the cotton gin did not even belong to Eli yet. He still had to get the government papers to prove it.

But one statement worried Eli most of all. Clean *any* amount of cotton? Building cotton gins by hand took time, lots of time. How could Miller and Whitney guarantee such a promise?

Phineas had just wanted to make sure that *everyone* grew cotton, he explained. April was planting time. So all Eli could do was make his machines and wait nervously for news of his patent.

Finally, on March 14, 1794, the patent was granted. Eli shared the good news with his father, inviting him to come and see his machines in New Haven. Six full-size gins were ready for shipment to Georgia, the proud inventor said.

By the middle of May, Eli also had a demonstration gin set up at Mulberry Grove. Kitty Greene's plantation spilled over with friends and neighbors eager to see the new invention. In one hour, the gin cleaned more cotton than several workers could do by hand in a whole day. Neighborhood boys summed up the wonder of Eli's machine, saying, "It's got teeth."

Whitney's creation was indeed a wonder, the cotton growers agreed. And so simple that anyone could make one. They had only one question. How soon would Miller and Whitney gins be ready to clean their cotton? As soon as he could build them, Eli assured them. The plantation owners hurried home to plant bumper crops of cotton.

Eli had planned to return in a few weeks to New Haven to make more gins, but an attack of malaria delayed him. Summer was nearly over before he was strong enough to travel north to his workshop. Back in Georgia, Phineas attended to setting up the gins and hiring managers and workers. According to Phineas's calculations, they would need fifty or sixty of Eli's finely crafted cotton-cleaning machines. All through the fall and winter, Eli and a team of workers labored over gins.

Then came the springtime of 1795. Eli had gone to New York, trying to get loans. It seemed like he always needed more money to build his gins. But then he was struck with another attack of malaria, delaying his return to the workshop. On the morning of March 11, while Eli recovered in New York, his workers back in New Haven were having breakfast. Suddenly, a worker shouted, "FIRE! FIRE!" The workshop was ablaze.

Eli came home to the terrible news. All of his hand-made tools, all of the machines that he had invented and only he could make, were gone. The coils of expensive wire, the stacks of fine wood, the seventeen gins that were nearly completed and others that had just been started, were gone. Everything was gone. It had all begun when the broom sitting by the hearth caught fire, a worker said sadly.

And there was more bad news, this time from Phineas. Georgia's fields had been snowy with cotton last fall, Phineas wrote. Planters had gotten tired of waiting for the promised gins. They were building gins of their own. When Phineas had called for the planters to stop using the illegal copycat gins, the makers of the copycats were irritated. They spread a cruel lie all over Georgia, saying that cotton from Eli's gins ruined spinning machines. The rumor was hurting business.

Eli was not discouraged. He knew his gins were the best. In seven months, his workshop was up and going again. He made twenty-six more of his finely crafted gins for America's growing cotton industry.

But by the beginning of 1796, the South was peppered with copycat gins. Miller and Whitney had no choice but to take the makers of the copies to court for disobeying the patent law.

Eli's and Phineas's hopes of winning were low. The courts they would face were all in cotton country. Many of the judges and juries were southern cotton growers themselves. They were not likely to take the side of Eli, an inventor from the North.

In May 1797, Miller and Whitney suffered a stunning defeat. The courts decided not to stop the cotton growers from making copycat gins. Business for Eli and Phineas came to a standstill. It looked as though Miller and Whitney were finished.

Penniless, defeated, deeply in debt, Eli returned to New Haven. Phineas promised to take care of the legal problems as best he could. In the meantime, he had the running of Mulberry Grove to keep him busy.

But Eli had dedicated himself to his work on the cotton gin, 100 percent. He was devastated. How could he tell his workers they no longer had jobs? How could he, an honorable Whitney, walk the streets of his college town, disgraced? How could he call himself an inventor?

For the first time in his life, Eli Whitney stopped believing in his gift for making things. Deep in the dark clouds of depression, he closed himself up in his New Haven boardinghouse room. Never again, he said, would he patent an invention.

4

Calamity after Calamity

The news spread quickly. Eli Whitney was back in town. But the good people of New Haven were worried. No longer did they see the cheery Eli they had once known walking the Green, a grassy square on Yale's campus. Invitations to social get-togethers went unanswered.

Staying cooped up in his room was no good, a worried buddy from Eli's Yale days wrote. Eli should get out, get some exercise, and have some fun. He should take courage and strike out on a new invention that would astonish the world. It was good advice, Eli admitted. But he could not bring himself to follow it.

One night in December 1797, a newspaper article caught Eli's eye. The U.S. government had approved money for muskets—40,000 of them. The United States was on the verge of war with France. America was desperately in need of muskets.

Muskets. The word stirred memories of Eli's boyhood days, watching neighbors marching off to war with only their turkey-shooting guns for protection. He remembered the blacksmiths' shops, crowded with muskets needing to be repaired.

That was the thing about muskets. There was no rushing the making of a musket. There was no rushing the training of musket makers, either. Where, Eli asked himself, did the government think it was going to get all those muskets? Not from its old friend France. Times had changed.

In the stillness of the winter's night, Eli Whitney sat thinking. He thought about the young United States of America. He thought about the freedom it had won so bravely, with the help of outdated Charleville muskets from France. Should America be manufacturing its own muskets? Eli thought of the questions he had asked in his Yale essays.

Eli thought about making things in America. Wagon wheels and chairs, hatpins and nails, cotton gins and muskets—just about everything was made by hand. Made by hands that differed in skill and by eyes that differed in sharpness, slowing the process to a turtle's pace. In Eli's mind, a squiggle of an idea began to take shape. Suppose—just suppose—those 40,000 muskets could be made by machines?

On January's sparkling mornings, Eli tramped about the town of New Haven. The best thing about crunching along in freshly fallen snow was that it started him pondering. How good it was to be pondering again!

All winter long, Eli thought about muskets. He thought about their makers and all they had to be. A gunsmith had to be part blacksmith, hammering gun barrels from pieces of white-hot metal. He had to be part foundry man, casting metal fittings. He had to be a welder fusing shapes together and a carver of wood and bone.

Eli would have to build machines to take over all of those jobs. Not only would he have to build them, he would have to invent them. Well, he had invented a machine that took the place of human fingers, had he not? Why could he not also make machines that took the place of hands and eyes?

On May 1, 1798, Eli sent a letter to Oliver Wolcott, who was still secretary of the treasury. Wolcott was keenly interested in American invention. He had once shown interest in Eli's cotton gin. This time, Eli had a new proposal. He would like to make 10,000 to 15,000 muskets for the U.S. government. The inventor made his intentions very clear. He told Wolcott that he planned to replace handmade muskets with machine-made muskets. He would produce thousands of muskets at a time.

Thousands at a time! Eli had not made even a single musket, let alone thousands. He believed he could, though.

The secretary of the treasury was not so sure. The U.S. Armory had been operating for three years. It had turned out a mere 900 muskets.

But those guns had been made by hand, Eli pointed out. His muskets would be made speedily, by machine. Time was short. The war with France was looming.

Eli's argument worked. On June 14, the contract was signed. Eli Whitney would supply the government with 10,000 machine-made muskets, to be delivered in two years' time. Payment would be $13.40 per musket. In the meantime, the government would lend him some money to get started.

Eli's heart beat fast with joy. He had a contract worth $134,000. He had the promise of $5,000 to help him begin. Boldly, Eli made a promise of his own. He would present the first 4,000 muskets by September 30, 1799, just a little more than one year away. The other 6,000 muskets would arrive by September 1800.

No sooner had the happy inventor begun his new

business venture, however, than the usual calamities began to set in. Eli had planned to buy the iron for the musket barrels in Philadelphia. He had also ordered a boat to carry 4,000 wooden gun stocks that the government was going to supply. The gun stocks had to travel from a Philadelphia warehouse to New Haven. The shipment had to happen before winter, when the Delaware River would freeze over.

But when August came, yellow fever hit Philadelphia again. The city shut down. Nothing could go in or out of its ports. Eli would not get his supplies any time soon.

Eli turned to another part of his carefully thought-out plan. He intended to build a factory at Mill Rock, just outside of New Haven. The property had a thirty-five-foot-high waterfall that would make the power for his musket-making machines. But buying the land and getting permission to use the waterfall took longer than Eli had expected. Then winter set in early with a fierce snowstorm. Eleven more record-breaking snows followed fast on its heels. The plaster walls of the new factory would not dry. Shivering workers could barely use their tools. It was January before Eli's workshop was completed.

Seven months had passed since Eli had signed the government contract. And he was nowhere near ready to begin making muskets. He still had to build many machines: one for drilling, one for boring musket barrels, and others for hammering, cutting, grinding, and polishing. For every step of musket making, Eli had to make a machine.

And still the materials from Philadelphia had not arrived. Eli searched all the nearby forges for the high-quality iron he desired. At last, he found a supplier who could fill his order. Within two weeks, the man promised. Two weeks went by and then a month. The iron did not appear. Finally, Eli got a message from the forge's owner. His forge had been damaged by a flood. He would not be able to fulfill the order. Worriedly, Eli arranged for shipment from a different forge.

In the meantime, Eli hired workers. Interviewing the sixty or so men he needed took lots of time. Eli wanted to be sure that his workers were serious about learning this new way of making muskets. He also wanted workers who would stay on the job. Eli had a dream. The Whitney Armory would offer a new way of life for factory workers in America. When all the factory buildings were completed, he planned to build a whole village. It would include houses for workers with families, a boardinghouse for single men, and a farm for producing food.

Eli's dream for a mill village left no detail untouched. The farm's barn would even have special Whitney-designed halters for the cattle. Some halters made it hard for animals to turn their heads. But Eli's were made so that the animals could always move their heads with perfect ease. Eli had not forgotten those long-gone days spent feeding his father's cattle.

At last, the fierce winter came to an end. The Whitney Armory's musket makers reported for work. Slowly, patiently, Eli began their training. None of the workers were trained gunsmiths. Teaching them his method of making muskets took time, lots of time. Eli found that he had to demonstrate how he wanted things done every step of the way.

The most complicated part of the job was making the lock, the combination of oddly shaped metal pieces that made the musket fire. For each and every piece of the lock, Eli had made a pattern. Workers followed the patterns to cut out pieces of metal.

Eli had also made machines to help the workers. A filing fixture held the metal in place. A filing jig guided the cutter's hands. Each time a worker cut that pattern, the musket piece he made would turn out exactly the same.

Summer came. The government was already expecting its first 4,000 muskets in just three months.

And the Whitney Armory had not yet completed a single musket!

Eli wrote to Secretary Wolcott, begging for more time. Setting up the new business had taken far longer than he had expected, Whitney explained. Teaching his workers had taken more time than he ever dreamed it would. The severe winter had delayed everything. He did not have all of his machines in place yet. Actually, the inventor admitted, the business was just getting going. And to top it all off, he was out of money.

Secretary Wolcott was worried. Was this bold new method of making muskets no more than a hazy idea in the inventor's head? Eli Whitney had seemed so honorable. Wolcott had one question. Did Eli honestly believe he could fulfill the contract?

Nothing could make him, an honorable Whitney, go back on his promise, Eli replied earnestly. Wolcott believed him. He agreed to give Eli more time, along with another $15,000 from the government.

September 1800 came and went without the U.S. government seeing a single musket. In November Eli received an official-looking envelope in the mail. The letter inside was signed by Samuel Dexter, the new secretary of the treasury. Wolcott, Eli's loyal supporter, was no longer in charge. Dexter had been looking over the records, the letter said. A lot of money had gone to the Whitney Armory. So where were those muskets?

Oliver Wolcott was gone. Who would speak for Eli Whitney now?

Not a soul, Eli decided. His machine-made muskets would have to speak for themselves.

In December Eli boarded a stagecoach and headed for Washington, D.C., the government's new capital. The evidence for Eli's case bumped along on the seat beside him.

5

Muskets for America

In the winter of 1801, an American inventor from the state of Connecticut stood before the officials of the U.S. government. Eli Whitney had promised to make 10,000 muskets for America, but not even one musket had been delivered.

But the muskets, those long-promised, machine-made guns, most certainly could be delivered, inventor Eli said firmly. There was good reason for his tardiness. Calamity after calamity had delayed the creation of his machines.

President John Adams and his stern-faced officials listened politely. Making machine-made muskets without machines would be most difficult. According to Eli, Whitney-made machines could turn out muskets by the thousands. In fact, the Whitney Armory was overflowing with muskets, nearly completed.

But why, asked the government men, should they keep handing out money to a musket maker whose muskets failed to appear?

A congressman sat listening. It was Elizur Goodrich Jr. Elizur's heart went out to his boyhood friend. Thomas Jefferson was there too. Jefferson, who had been one of the biggest supporters of Eli's cotton gin. Jefferson, who was running for president.

Eli took courage from having such important supporters. Boldly, he launched into his argument. Behold Exhibit A, he said—a completed machine-made musket. The government men's eyebrows went up. So the inventor's machines *could* make muskets, after all.

Eli continued. The gentlemen were familiar with muskets, were they not? The government men nodded their heads knowingly. But how many knew that a musket was a very complicated machine? Eli asked. The government men's eyes stared blankly.

A musket, Eli explained, was made up of fifty pieces. The most complicated piece was the lock. Ever since times gone by, locks were chiseled out by hand. No two locks turned out exactly the same.

But, said Eli, thanks to his new way of making muskets, locks could be shaped by machine. Every one could come out exactly alike.

Thomas Jefferson looked interested. Samuel Dexter, secretary of the treasury, still looked doubtful. Using machines, added Eli, his voice as soft as cotton, would save the government money. Eli had not spent years debating at Yale for nothing.

The government men leaned closer. Gentlemen— Exhibit B. A pile of metal pieces clanked onto the table. Choosing at random from the pieces, Eli built a musket lock before their very eyes. Every piece snapped perfectly into place. Any worker, no matter how new, could easily assemble a machine-made lock, no matter how complicated, said Eli. Gentlemen—give it a try.

The government men stepped cautiously forward. Did Eli actually expect *them* to make something from those oddball hunks of metal on the table?

In minutes the men had their musket locks assembled. But Eli was not finished with his flabbergasted audience. The gentlemen were to disassemble their creations, take them apart, and exchange pieces with their fellow builders.

The lock builders quickly made a discovery. Any piece fit any lock. Every piece fit every lock! Eli's machine-made musket parts were totally interchangeable. Muskets, all just alike, could indeed be produced by machine.

The evidence was clear. With Eli's new way of making things, the United States would no longer have to depend upon the help of foreign countries to defend its freedom.

Eli pressed onward. There was still one catch in his method, he admitted, that slowed down the whole process. He did not have a machine that could pelt out the lock's oddly shaped pieces musket-fire quick. His workers still cut them out by hand. He could make that machine, though. And he could make improvements to the musket design, as well.

Eli was "the Artist of the Country," the government men proclaimed. He simply had to name his terms. What did he need from them?

Eli gave them a gentle Whitney smile. The improvements could be made quite easily, he said, with just a wee bit more time. And a wee bit more money would not hurt, either. An advance of $10,000 in February and another $5,000 in April would be a great help. A further $5,000 upon delivery of every 500 muskets, plus two and one-half years more for delivery, would complete the deal.

The government men nodded their heads in agreement. Their stern faces smiled. All but Samuel Dexter's. After all, it was Dexter who had to hand out the money.

But Eli's arguing had won the case. To top off his victory, his friend Congressman Goodrich had arranged a meeting with Thomas Jefferson. Perhaps Eli would like to come along?

At last, Eli and Thomas Jefferson would be able to talk. Jefferson was full of praise for Eli's new method of manufacture. In no instance, he said, had he seen workmanship equal to Eli's, except, perhaps, in France. A skillful gunsmith there named Le Blanc had produced work of similar quality. Jefferson looked thoughtful. Could Eli Whitney be America's Le Blanc?

Eli returned to Mill Rock with a light heart. He had three times the amount of money named in his original contract. His schedule had stretched to five years. He also had the support—and friendship—of Thomas Jefferson, who was both a kindred spirit and one of the most influential people in America. The Whitney Armory was on the road to success.

It was a good thing that Eli was on his way to finishing his muskets for America. The war with France had not happened after all. But now America was on the verge of war with Great Britain. British ships were capturing American ships, sailors, and goods. Thomas Jefferson was worried. He had become President Jefferson, and he wanted to avoid war.

But if he could not, America had best be prepared. Meanwhile, Eli was having to pester Samuel Dexter for the money he needed. How could there be muskets if the musket maker didn't have any money?

President Jefferson had an idea. He decided to make the musket contract the responsibility of the war department, instead of the treasury department. Eli began dealing with the secretary of war, Henry Dearborn. Dearborn had a lot of military experience. He knew what the American army needed. It needed well-made muskets, regardless of the cost or time. He made sure that Eli got the money he needed.

Finally, one fine September day in 1801, Eli had a wonderful surprise for his ten-year-old nephew, Philos Blake. Philos, the son of Eli's sister, Elizabeth, had come to live with his uncle. Uncle Eli had all sorts of marvelous new machines, Philos eagerly wrote home. But today's surprise was even more impressive. Uncle's workshop held 500 machine-made muskets, complete and ready for shipment.

On September 26, 1801, the 500 Whitney-made muskets were delivered to the U.S. government. Shipments from the Whitney Armory flowed steadily in lots of 500 from that day on.

On January 23, 1809, Eli Whitney informed the secretary of war that the last of the promised 10,000 muskets were complete and ready for government inspection. The delivery came at a good time. In March James Madison became the fourth president of the United States. The new president's first talk to the nation was serious. Great Britain and America remained on the very brink of war.

Thanks to Eli, the soldiers fighting the War of 1812 (also called the Second War for Independence) carried spiffy new American-made muskets. When all was said and done, Eli made just $2,450 profit from the deal. But he had fulfilled his contract. The Whitney Armory was a success.

Was there anything that could make Eli's success more complete? Just one thing. Eli longed to get back to inventing. He had not forgotten the bottle-neck that slowed down his musket manufacture. And he had an idea.

6

Man of Ideas

Eli's idea was with him when he sat down to quiet dinnertime talks with his friend Thomas Jefferson. It followed him in and out of the cow barn with the specially designed cattle halters. Whirling in inventor Eli's mind in 1817 was an idea that would totally change manufacturing in America.

Eli's idea was to make a milling machine that would cut metal more precisely than could be done by hand. The milling machine would have rotating metal teeth.

These teeth would be able to trace and cut any pattern, no matter how unusual the shape. The piece of metal to be cut would be clamped to a table. The pattern to be followed would be placed on top of this metal plate, and then a water-powered cutting tool would follow the pattern.

Eli's milling machine finally made it possible for the most intricate pieces of the musket to be made musket-fire quick. But Eli did not apply for a patent to protect his idea. Instead, he chose to make his new invention available to other armories that made muskets for America. And anyone who wanted to visit the Whitney Armory was welcome to come and see the work going on there.

Thanks to Eli, manufacturing muskets and other products in America had changed dramatically. The process of making all of these things could become faster, less expensive, and more accurate than it had ever been before.

Eli had passed his fiftieth birthday. He was happy with his success as an inventor. But he realized that there was still an empty spot in his heart that no amount of business could fill. Eli longed for a family of his own. On January 6, 1817, he married Henrietta Edwards, the daughter of a respected New Haven judge.

Henrietta had long admired the gentle inventor. She and Eli celebrated their wedding with a small party. Friends congratulated the joyful couple.

Marriage brought new happiness into Eli's life. Later, Eli's joy grew with the birth of his four children, Fanny, Elizabeth, Eli Jr., and Susan.

Sadly, the children's father was not very well during the later years of his life. Eli spent many days in bed. There was always a sketchpad nearby. Father might not be feeling quite up to par, but he still had plenty of time for pondering. Often, the children kept him company. They cast longing eyes at their father's dresser drawers. What treasures might be hiding inside? Pennies for candy? A pocket watch?

A shiny new key soon appeared on the dresser. Eli's new invention was a mysterious system of locks. Only when the key was turned in the top dresser drawer would the other drawers magically open as well. But boys and girls with a passion for dissecting any curious little machines inside first had to master the puzzle. When Eli died in 1825, he left behind many wonderful puzzles—and young minds eager to solve them.

More about Eli Whitney

Eli Whitney was born on December 8, 1765, one month after the first British tax was placed on the American colonies. Taxes such as these eventually led to the American Revolution.

Many people can and do claim to have invented the cotton gin. Other inventors in Eli's time were making improved roller gins. Later, in about 1857, a Mississippi slave known only as Ned invented a labor-saving device he called a cotton scraper. But neither slaves nor their masters could apply for patents. Eli Whitney is remembered as the first inventor to have an official patent on the cotton gin.

In addition to his work on the cotton gin and the mass-produced musket, Eli made many improvements to the rifle and to a variety of machine tools.

Eli Whitney, pioneer of mass manufacture in America, died on January 8, 1825. His friend and supporter Thomas Jefferson died a year and a half later, on the Fourth of July, 1826.

After Eli's death, his nephews Philos Whitney Blake and Eli Whitney Blake carried on their uncle's business. A model of Eli's mill village, along with exhibits depicting his life and contributions to manufacture in America, can still be explored at the Whitney Museum in Hamden, Connecticut.

Selected Bibliography

Earle, Alice Morse. *Home Life in Colonial Days.* New York: Grosset and Dunlop, 1974.

"Eli Whitney." *Virtualology.com.* 2001. <http://www.virtualology.com/eli-whitney.org> (June 2, 2003).

"Eli Whitney, Inventor of the Cotton Gin." *The Whitney Research Group.* 1999. <http://www.whitneygen.org/archives/biography/eli.html> (June 2, 2003).

Eli Whitney Museum. N.d. <http://www.eliwhitney.org> (June 2, 2003).

Green, Constance McLaughlin. *Eli Whitney and the Birth of American Technology.* Boston: Little Brown, 1956.

Mirsky, Jeannette, and Allen Nevins. *The World of Eli Whitney.* New York: The MacMillan Company, 1952.

Moorshead, Halvor. "Eli Whitney." *History Magazine,* June/July 2000, 15–16.

Taylor, Dale. *Everyday Life in Colonial America.* Cincinnati, OH: Writer's Digest Books, 1997.

Trussell, John B. B. *Birthplace of an Army: A Study of the Valley Forge Encampment.* Harrisburg, PA: Commonwealth of Pennsylvania, Pennsylvania Historical and Museum Commission, 1976.

Index

About the Author

Barbara Mitchell grew up in Chester, Pennsylvania, where she happily hammered out creations in her patternmaker father's pine-smelling workshop. Her father made pine and expensive mahogany patterns for castings of steel that became airplanes and locomotives.

All the family members were readers. When Barbara's brother George Cornog took over the family business, he swiftly installed a bookshelf. The workers deserved a good read on their breaks, he said. Tucked among the selections are Barbara's twenty-some books for young readers.

About the Illustrator

Jan Naimo Jones has been a professional illustrator for twenty-five years. She studied illustration at Kendall School of Design, and she has worked on many books for young people. She has also been an elementary-school art teacher and a mural painter at homes and churches. She lives in Grand Rapids, Michigan, where her art and her seven kids keep her very busy.